KU-555-435

Grantham House

EX LIBRIS

GH

Volume Two

Classic Railcars, Electric & Diesel Locomotives
of New Zealand

On 20 July 1993, just five months short of the 130th anniversary of railways in New Zealand, the Government announced that the state-owned company had been sold to a consortium led by the United States railway company Wisconsin Central. The other members of the consortium were the US investment company Berkshire Partners and the New Zealand merchant banker Fay Richwhite. The sale included the trains, tracks, bridges and tunnels, stations and workshops and the rail ferries, but not the land, which remains state-owned through the Railways Corporation.
Fay Richwhite declared their intention to sell down their 40 per-cent shareholding within a few years, enabling New Zealand investors to buy a stake in what is one of the very few railways of its kind to achieve financial success.

/3

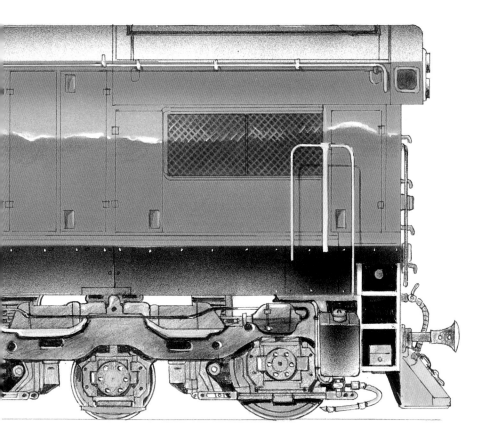

Volume Two

Classic Railcars, Electric & Diesel Locomotives
of New Zealand

Eric Heath

Text by Bob Stott

Grantham House

New Zealand

Also by Eric Heath
New Zealand Sea Anglers' Guide (with Ray Doogue and John Moreland)
Whales of New Zealand (with Bernard Stonehouse)
Butterflies of New Zealand (with John Salmon)
Sharks of New Zealand (with J.A.F. Garrick)
Gulls and Terns of New Zealand (with Bernard Stonehouse)
Marine Fishes of New Zealand No. 1 (with John Moreland)
New Zealand Farm Pests in Colour (with A.D. Lowe)
Seashore Life in New Zealand (with R.K. Dell)
Ferns and Fern Allies in New Zealand (with R.J. Chinnock)
Common Insects of New Zealand (with Annette Walker)
Marine Fishes of New Zealand No. 2 (with Larry Paul)

Also by Bob Stott
Rails Through the Bush
Twilight of Trams (with A.C. Bellamy)
Kaimai
NZ Railway Album
Cook Strait Ferry Story
Bush Tram to the Mill
NZ Railway Wagons
Prices of Thames
NIMT 75th Anniversary Album
Rimutaka Incline Yesterday & Today
NZ Railways The first 125 Years (with D.B. Leitch)

First published 1993

GRANTHAM HOUSE PUBLISHING

P.O. Box 17-256
Wellington 5
New Zealand

© Eric Heath.
Text Bob Stott

All rights reserved.
No part of this publication may be reproduced, stored in a retrieval
system or transmitted in any form or by any means, electronic,
mechanical, photocopying, recording or otherwise, without the prior
written permission of the publisher.

ISBN 1 86934 041 8

Edited by Anna Rogers
Typeset by Setrite Typesetters, Hong Kong
Designed by Bookprint Consultants Limited, Wellington
Printed by Kings Time Printing Press of Hong Kong in association with
Bookprint Consultants Limited, Wellington

Acknowledgements

I am very grateful to all the people who have helped me with the preparation of this book. I would like to thank Tom McGavin for compiling the list of locomotives and railcars and his help with many photographs and drawings; Peter Dyer, retired mechanical engineer, New Zealand Rail Ltd for checking the details of each engine; Brian Rudman of the Electric Multiple Unit Depot, Wellington; the staffs of the Diesel Depot, Wellington and the Electric Locomotive Depot, Palmerston North; Alastair Horsfield, Transtec, Lower Hutt; the staff of Hutt Workshops; Noel Kerrisk, formerly Corporate Relations Manager, New Zealand Rail Ltd; Albert Bossward, Locomotive Maintenance Engineer, New Zealand Rail Ltd; the staff of National Archives; and John Heap.

I would also like to thank Steam Incorporated, Paekakariki; Silver Stream Railway Incorporated, Hutt Valley; Ferrymead Railway, Christchurch; Ashburton Railway and Preservation Society Incorporated; and Pleasant Point Railway and Historical Society, South Canterbury.

Finally, thanks to Bob Stott, editor of *Rails*, for the text, his help with photographs and plans, and for patiently answering many telephone calls.

Contents

Introduction

Almost 90 years after the first steam locomotive rolled down the track in New Zealand, this small South Pacific nation saw its first main line diesel electric locomotive, and even then the pioneer DE class was originally intended for heavy shunting work. Two years later, the first true main line diesel electric, the 1500 hp DF, went into service on the North Island Main Trunk line.

Electric traction has a longer history. It was 1923 when the pioneer EO class started work on the line through the 8.5 km Otira tunnel under the Southern Alps. As the the climb through the tunnel is as steep as 1 in 33, electric traction was the only practical choice. Other electrification schemes followed through the Lyttelton tunnel to Christchurch in 1929 and on Wellington's suburban Johnsoville branch in 1938. Eventually all suburban lines radiating from Wellington would be electrified.

These were all short sections; long distance main line electrification had to wait until 1988 with the completion of the electrification of the central portion of the North Island Main Trunk between Hamilton and Palmerston North. The NIMT scheme, unlike its 1500 v dc predecessors, utilised the modern 25 kV ac system.

Although not strictly locomotives, railcars and electric multiple units are also included in these pages. After all, like locomotives they are self-propelled, and anyway they are interesting machines in their own right. New Zealand Railway was well up with the play in the early days of railcar development. As early as 1912, a petrol electric car was tried out, and a variety of others, including two different types of steam railcar, a battery electric and other internal combution-powered machines, were experimented with. The results ranged from outright failure to near-miss, but in 1936 NZR got it right with a small fleet of railcars built in its own workshops for the Wairarapa service, a route which included the demanding Fell-worked Rimutaka Incline.

Notwithstanding their success, most subsequent railcar types were imported from overseas, as have been the two classes of electric multiple unit trains for Wellington's suburban rail system, and the recently acquired diesel multiple units for Auckland suburban lines.

Steam traction on NZR ended in 1967 in the North Island and in 1971 in the South, although in the final years only a handful of trains were steam-hauled, and then only to supply heat to the steam-heated carriages of those days.

With steam's demise, the end of public interest in railways was forecast, for who could enthuse over mass-produced and colourless diesels and electrics? They were wrong, of course, and New Zealand, like every other developed country, still has a network of railway enthusiasts and railway museums which show as much interest in diesels and electric as in their steam-powered predecessors. Proof of this claim lies in the fact that at least one of every main line diesel and electric of past years has been preserved.

As outlined in the first volume of this work, New Zealand Railways in steam days achieved a very high level of self-sufficiency in meeting its motive power requirements. There were few such small and isolated systems capable of building

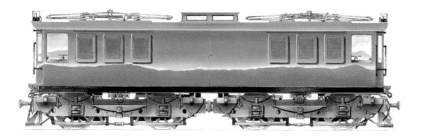

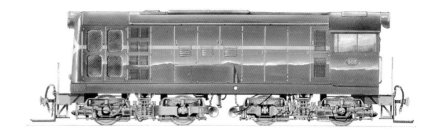

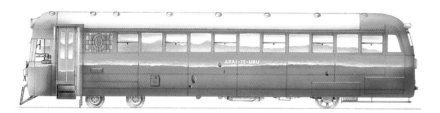

modern steam locomotives in fleet-sized numbers and New Zealand was one of that select few.

With the inevitable switch to non-steam motive power, NZR did not re-equip its workshops to build fleets of diesels, for the modern locomotive is so complicated and sophisticated that mass production is essential to keep production costs at a level that operators can afford. So NZR went shopping overseas for its non-steam motive power, at first to Britain and then more recently to the United States, a pattern rather similar to that which unfolded in steam days.

Most of the diesel electrics imported into New Zealand have been based on existing designs, as the world's big locomotive makers have stock 'export' models which can be supplied to a variety of gauges and with a variety of features to suit the purchaser's requirements. Nevertheless, there is a sort of 'family' resemblance between the various diesel classes, the style setter being the DC class rebuilds described in these pages.

But no matter what they look like, the various classes of non-steam motive power still hold the enthusiast's interest, and the withdrawal of a particular class from service is marked by special excursions, many photographs, a good deal of nostalgia and then the inevitable selection of one of the type for preservation.

This book describes and illustrates the most significant of the various diesel and electric locomotives and railcars to run in New Zealand, many of which are still out on the line earning money for their masters. So, unlike the companion steam locomotive volume, this book offers a story which has no end, because the railway continues to evolve and, as it does, New Zealand Rail continues to develop its motive power fleet to meet new demands.

The steam locomotive is dead, or at least consigned to museums and railways operated solely for pleasure, but the story of the diesels and electrics is a living one. In New Zealand, as overseas, railways will become increasingly important in the future as concerns about the environment, fuel supplies, congestion, and road safety again focus public attention on the rails. Look at this book, then, not as a neatly packaged slice of transport history, but as the story so far...

Class EO — 1923

Main line electric traction appeared quite early on NZR with the introduction of the five EO locomotives built by English Electric to haul trains through the 5.3-mile (8.6 km) Otira Tunnel under the Southern Alps. The electrified section extended only from Otira through the tunnel to Arthur's Pass, a distance of 8.6 miles (14 km), and until they were replaced by five new locomotives imported from Japan in 1968, the EO's spent all their life shuttling to and fro over this short section. However, as the grade through the tunnel was a steady 1 in 33 theirs was not an easy life; the combination of that grade plus the tunnel length also make it clear why steam traction was never contemplated for this section.

And so the EO's had something in common with the H class Fells — from the opening of the line they handled virtually all traffic offering and continued to do so until written off. In later years all regular passenger services through the tunnel were handled by diesel railcars, but the railways certainly got their money's worth from the EO's. As can be seen from the illustration, they were a double bogie box cab type, with the drawgear carried on the bogies, which in turn were linked together so that traction and buffing forces were not carried by the under-frame. In later years the locomotives were altered to a single cab design.

One EO locomotive is preserved at the Ferrymead Railway, Christchurch.
Specifications
Wheel arrangement: Bo+Bo
Weight: 50 tons (50.8 tonnes)
Traction motors: 4
Power output: 680 hp (507 kW)
Tractive effort: 14,160 lbs (63 kN)
Driving wheel diam.: 45 in (1143 mm) Length: 38 feet 6 inches (11.734 metres)

Class EC — 1929

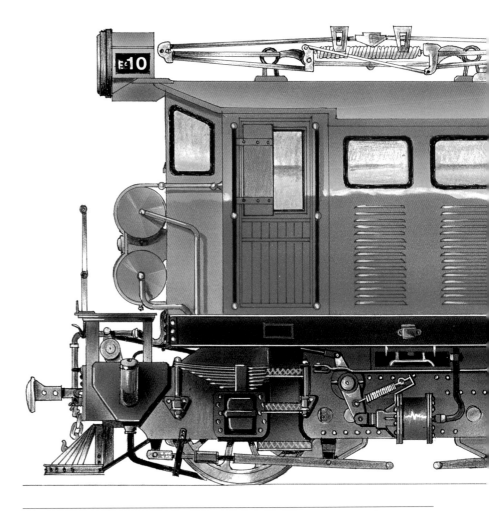

New Zealand Railways' second excursion into electric traction came six years after the EO (the 'o' was for Otira) class entered service through the Otira Tunnel. This second scheme again involved a tunnel, the 1.5-mile (2.4 km) Lyttelton Tunnel on the 6.8-mile (11 km) line linking the city of Christchurch with the port of Lyttelton. Classed EC ('c' for Christchurch), the new locomotives were quite similar to the EO's, being once again box cabs running on two four-wheeled bogies, and with cabs at each end. Six were built by English Electric, the aim being to eliminate the smoke nuisance caused by steam traction. Although the Lyttelton tunnel was much shorter than the Otira, and on only a slight grade, the line carried quite an intensive suburban pasenger train service as well as goods trains serving the port. To many eyes, the Ec was a more attractive locomotive than the EO, its angled cab front being decidedly European in character. These locomotives ran without any fuss for years until the opening of a road tunnel to Lyttelton in 1964 and then the advent of diesel traction paved the way for their withdrawal from service, and removal of the electrification equipment, from 1970. Today suburban services are worked by buses through the road tunnel and diesels haul goods trains through the rail tunnel.

One EC locomotive is preserved at the Ferrymead Railway, Christchurch.
Specifications
Wheel arrangement: Bo+Bo
Weight: 50 tons (50.8 tonnes)
Traction motors: 4
Power output: 1188 hp (886 kW)
Tractive effort: 11,600 lbs (52 kN)
Driving wheel diam.: 45 in (1143 mm)   Length: 39 feet 3 inches (11.963 metres)

Wairarapa Railcar — 1936

The self-propelled railcar has played an important part in the history of NZR, which is not surprising considering the country's small population and extensive network of lines — far easier to find railcar-sized passenger loads than whole trains full. The earliest experiment dates back to 1912 when a 12-seat, petrol engine-powered, four-wheeled car was built. This vehicle and eight successive designs proved to be either outright failures or only qualified successes; several, including a battery car, almost made it but none were worth multiplying into a fleet.

Then, in 1936, six large petrol-engined railcars were built at Hutt workshops for the Wellington-Wairarapa run, a route that include the 1 in 15 Rimutaka Incline. These were unusual vehicles, bus-like in appearance, running on four-wheeled front bogies and with single rear axles, the whole arranged to clear the incline centre rail. They seated 49 passengers, had luggage space and toilets, cut an hour off the Wellington-Masterton run and could cruise quite happily at 60 mph (100 km /h). Their 13.5-tonne weight and seating capacity were quite close to the railbus prototypes that appeared on overseas railways in the 1960s and 1970s. Their riding qualities were not perfect, owing to the single rear axle, but this was a small price to pay for what was otherwise a fast and comfortable car.

They were named after Maori canoes, later received replacement diesel engines and, after running up huge mileages, became redundant when the Rimutaka Tunnel opened in 1955, opening up the Wairarapa to the then standard 88-seat railcars.

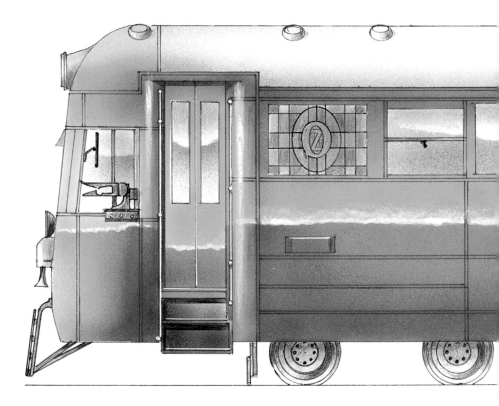

A Wairarapa railcar is preserved at Pahiatua.
Specifications
Engines (no., power): 1, 130 hp (97 kW)
Transmission: Diesel mechanical
Weight: 13.4 tons (13.6 tonnes)
Seats: 49   Length: 48 feet 9 inches (14.859 metres)

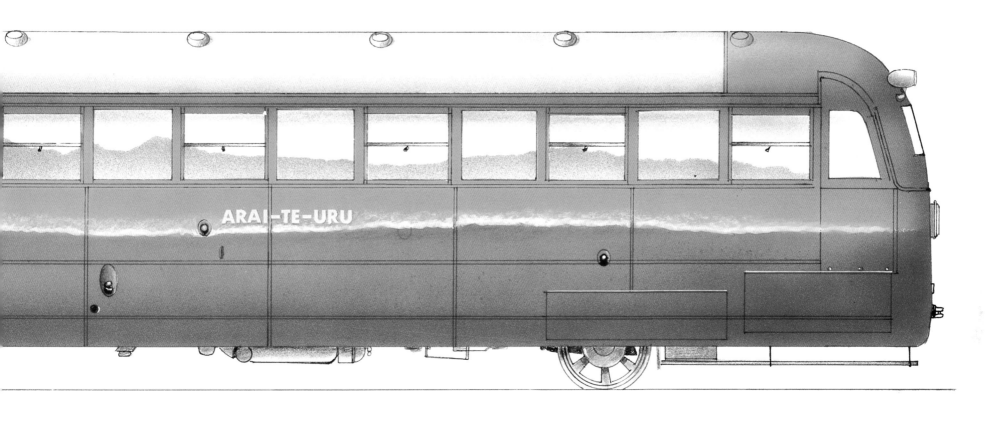

Standard Railcar — 1938

To years after the Wairarapa railcars arrived, the first of a new breed of railcar went into service — a double bogie design, streamlined in best 1930s style, and very much an express railcar. The new machines had cabs at each end, and an interesting feature of the design was that the two diesel engines which powered them were mounted on the bogies. They were painted in their own distinctive livery, as seen in the illustration, and again each was named after a famous Maori canoe. The first two railcars originally had first-class seats in the small compartments, the others of the six being second-class throughout. Seating capacities were 48 and 52 respectively. They went into service on the Wellington-Napier-Gisborne run and also on the Wellington-New Plymouth run, being concentrated on the latter route after being displaced from the Hawke's Bay line by the 88-seat railcars.

These were popular railcars, fast and quiet, and credited with reaching speeds of up to 75 mph (120 km/h) on trial. Before the last were retired in 1972, each of the six cars had worn out no fewer than three sets of diesel engines. Products, like their Wairarapa class predecessors, of NZR's Hutt workshops, these cars confirmed that NZR had the skills to build entirely reliable internal combustion-engined machines.

Sadly, the attractive livery did not last long. Motorists then, as today, had trouble identifying level crossings with rail traffic and protested that the railcars were too hard to see, so they were painted overall red like the Wairarapa cars. Later the red was relieved by broad silver flashes along the sides, a livery used on other railcars and on some main line diesel-electric locomotives.

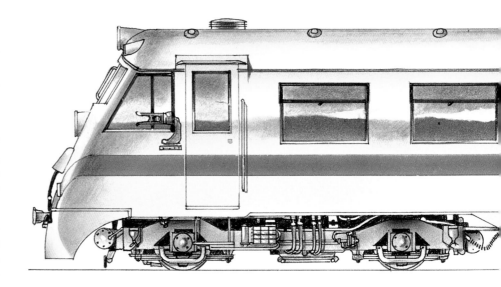

Two Standard railcars are preserved at the Silver Stream Railway, Hutt Valley, one at the Te Awamutu Railway Museum and one privately.
Specifications
Engines (no., power): 2, 230 hp total (171.6 kW)
Transmission: Diesel mechanical
Weight: 29.5 tons (30 tonnes)
Seats: 52   Length: 67 feet 11-1/2 inches (20.713 metres)

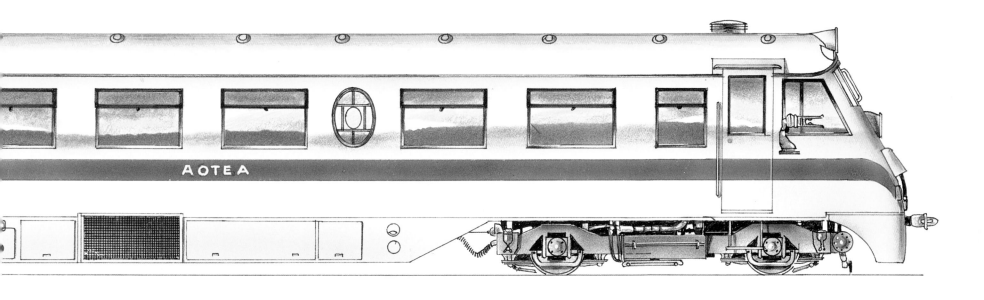

AOTEA

Class ED — 1939

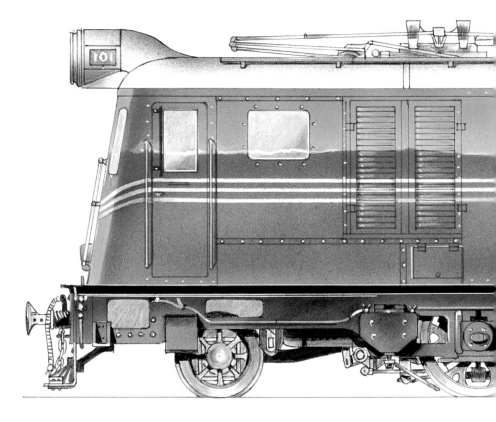

Wellington suburban lines were the third section of NZR to be electrified and, as at Otira and Christchurch, 1500V dc was selected. The first section was from Wellington to Johnsonville, once part of the North Island Main Trunk line and a dead end branch after the opening of the Tawa Flat deviation in 1937. Electric services worked by multiple unit trains were inaugurated the following year. It was also decided to electrify the new main line as far as Paekakariki, a section that included two long tunnels and a steep climb over the Pukerua saddle. The first ED locomotive was imported from English Electric, plus nine sets of equipment for the construction of additional locomotives in NZR's own Hutt and Addington shops.

Originally two ED's were stationed at Otira (the 'd' stood for 'duplicated' as they were at two sites — or so the story goes), but these two went north to Wellington during World War II. The ED's were of the 1-Do-2 wheel arrangement with the motors mounted on the main frame, linked by quill drive to the four central wheelsets. They had on-board steam boilers to supply steam heat to carriages but this equipment was later removed. The first ED, 101, had three bands of unpainted aluminium alloy along the body sides, as seen in the illustration. It also had deep side skirts that all but concealed the wheels, giving it a rather quaint look, but these were removed in the interests of accessibility.

Intended for both goods and passenger work, these were powerful locomotives but they rode as roughly as many a steam loco and were hard on the track, so a 45 mph (70 km/h) speed limit was imposed on them. Withdrawals started in 1969, with the last two going in 1981, but over this latter period they were used only when absolutely necessary. Why they were not built as Bo-Bo types is not entirely clear, although it does seem that there was in those days a reluctance to build higher horsepower motors into such bogie arrangements.

One ED is preserved at the Silver Stream Railway, Hutt Valley, and one at Ferrymead Railway, Christchurch

Specifications

Wheel arrangement: 1–Do–2
Weight: 86 tons (87 tonnes)
Traction motors: 4
Power output: 1240 hp (925 kW)
Tractive effort: 18,000 lbs (80 kN)
Driving wheel diam.: 45 in (1143 mm)   Length: 46 feet 2 inches (14.072 metres)

Vulcan Railcars — 1940

Such was the success of the Standard railcars on provincial lines in the North Island that a decision was made to put a similar type of vehicle into service in the south. It might be thought that the so-called Standard car would also become the South Island standard, but, owing to very full programmes in the NZR workshops, an order for 10 bogie diesel cars was placed with the Vulcan Foundry in England. The new machines were radically different from the Standards. Each had a four-wheeled bogie at one end and a six-wheeled bogie at the other, with the engine mounted above the floor in its own compartment above the six-wheeled bogie. The cars seated 50 in two compartments, with a central entrance. One railcar was lost at sea when the ship bringing it to New Zealand fell victim to a German submarine attack.

The Vulcans worked most South Island routes over the years — the Midland line west of Christchurch, the North line to Picton, the Main Trunk and the Otago Central all saw these cars in regular service at different times. It is worth noting that on trial in 1940 one car reached a speed of 78 mph (125.5 km/h), which appears to be the highest 'official' speed recorded on NZR. All were withdrawn by 1978.

There are three preserved Vulcan railcars at the Ferrymead Railway, Christchurch and one at the Plains Railway, Ashburton.
Specifications (1940)
Engines (no., power): 1, 250.8 hp (187 kW)
Transmission: Diesel mechanical
Weight: 36.2 tons (36.8 tonnes)
Seats: 48   Length: 68 feet 3 inches (20.803 metres)

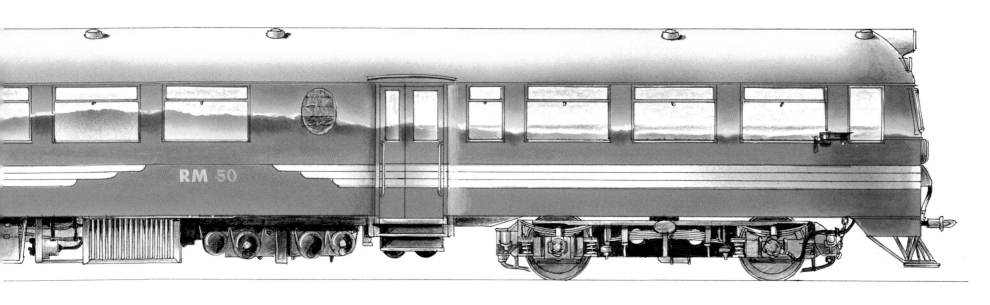

RM 50

Class D/DM — 1949

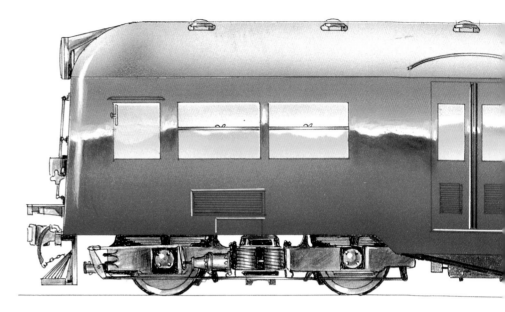

The Wellington to Johnsonville branch line was electrified and all services were taken over by multiple unit trains in 1938. After World War II it was decided to press on with electrifying the other suburban lines around the capital and an order was placed with the makers of the first batch of units, English Electric, for a further 40 DM class motor coaches and 71 D class trailer coaches. The new arrivals which went into service from 1949 varied in a number of minor details from the original six DM and six D cars bought for Johnsonville (supplemented by three more DM's and two D's in 1946). The new cars were normally operated in three-car units (trailer-motor-trailer) and took over services to Paekakariki, Upper Hutt and Melling as the overhead reached these termini.

These cars must be numbered among the list of real successes — they have proved reliable and economical machines over more than four decades. The earliest Johnsonville type cars were scrapped after some 40 years' service, and many of the 1949 units have also gone now, displaced by the newer Ganz Mavag cars. But even today a few peak-time sets are still worked by the 'old reds', now in their fifth decade of operation. A few English Electric sets were refurbished and painted in the Ganz Mavag livery of green and cream for the Johnsonville line. Concerns about limited clearances on that line were the reason for retaining this small fleet. Recent clearance tests, however, have indicated that Johnsonville, too, might yet become a Ganz Mavag route.

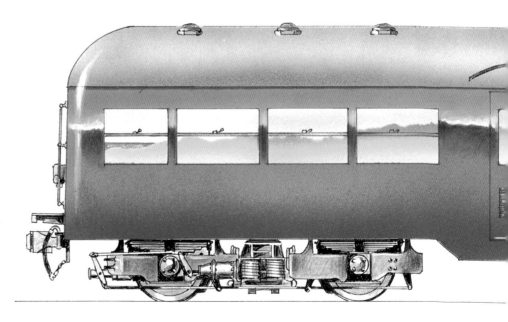

A DM and a D are preserved at the Ferrymead Railway, Christchurch.
Specifications
Traction motors (no., power): 4, 599.4 hp total (447 kW)
Weight: DM, 42.8 tons (43.5 tonnes); D, 27 tons (27.4 tonnes)
Seats: DM, 56; D, 72   Length: 62 feet 2 inches (19.152 metres)

Class DS — 1949

From the beginning, railway yards in New Zealand were shunted by superannuated main line locomotives; only the C Class 2-6-2s of 1930 could be described as being designed specifically for yard work. For light shunting, so-called shunting tractors had been used for some years. Although these were so low-powered that engine drivers conceded they could be operated by Traffic Branch staff, they proved as economical as the aged steam locomotives proved costly. The solution for heavier shunting work lay in modern diesel shunters, preferably off-the-shelf models, which could work around the clock and cost much less in fuel and manpower than steam traction.

Just such a machine was the DS, a sturdy 0-6-0 diesel mechanical from Drewry of England, built to that company's standard designs. The DS soon showed that it could shift up to 1000 tonnes at slow speeds, and work 24-hour shifts if need be. Initially four went into service at Wellington, then came another seven, followed by a third, heavier batch classed DSA. Other orders from different suppliers followed over the years so that shunting was soon dominated by D series 0-6-0s.

In the end the rigid wheelbase locomotives were displaced from the heaviest work by double bogie machines. The breed was almost extinct by the end of the decade of the 1980s and today none remain in regular use. Interestingly, however, there is still a limited role for some of the small shunting tractors, so side-rod drive has not yet vanished from NZR.

Preserved DS locomotives are at Steam Incorporated, Paekakariki; the Ocean Beach Railway, Dunedin; and the Glenbrook Vintage Railway, South Auckland.
Specifications
Wheel arrangement: 0−6−0
Weight: 25.5 tons (26 tonnes)
Diesel engine power output: 204 hp (152 kW)
Driving wheel diam.: $39\frac{3}{4}$ in (1010 mm)   Length: 25 feet 8 inches (7.823 metres)

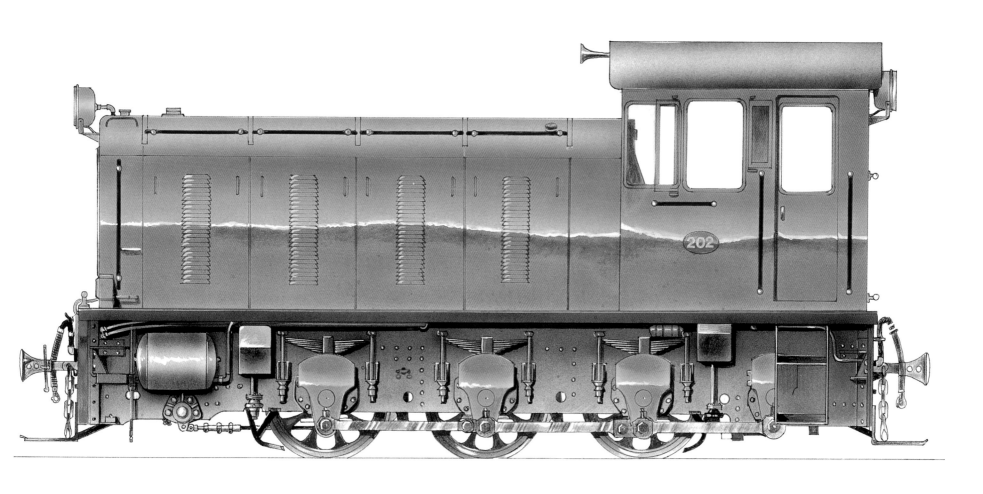

Class DE — 1952

New Zealand Railways entered the age of the diesel electric locomotive with the delivery of the first of the 15 DE's. Built by English Electric, these machines were intended for shunting in major yards but in their early days they ran main line goods trains in the Wairarapa, hauled heavy suburban trains in the Wellington area and even worked the 1953 Royal Tour trains in the North Island. Some went to Auckland for suburban train service there and others hauled log trains in the early days of the Murupara-Kawerau line. In the end they were confined largely to shunting in main yards, which is what they were designed to do.

After a long and useful life, all the DE's were written off by 1989, but New Zealand Rail has retained one in its small collection of historic locomotives and rolling stock. And it is not a static exhibit but, restored to original livery, a shunter at Wellington locomotive depot.

A DE has been preserved by New Zealand Rail, and others by the Otago Excursion Train Trust, Dunedin; the Silver Stream Railway, Hutt Valley; the Glenbrook Vintage Railway, South Auckland (2); and the Diesel Traction Group, Ferrymead, Christchurch (2).

Specifications (1964)
Wheel arrangement: Bo−Bo
Weight: 51 tons (52 tonnes)
Diesel engine output: 660 hp (492 kW)
Traction motors: 4
Tractive effort: 12,700 lbs (56 kN)
Diam. of driving wheels: 36.5 in (927 mm)   Length: 38 feet 3 inches (11.658 metres)

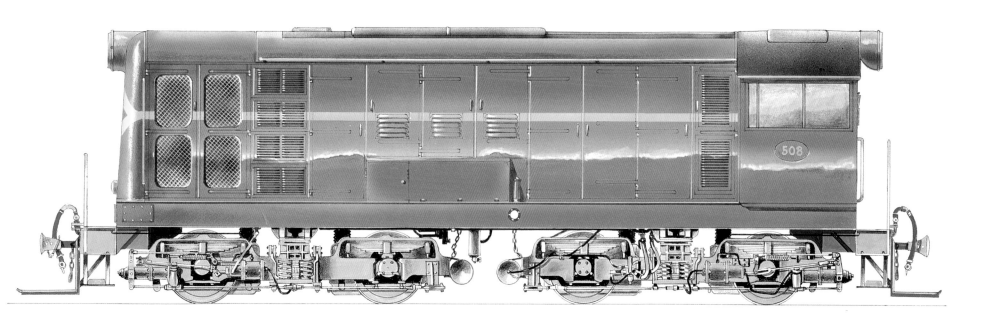

Class EW — 1952

For almost two decades the most powerful locomotives on NZR, the EW's were also among the most handsome machines to grace the railway. Although built by English Electric, the seven EW's were decidedly European in design, even to the triple bogie articulated format. They were ordered at a time when the Wellington area 1500V dc electrification was being extended to Upper Hutt and to Melling, the Johnsonville and Paekakariki lines having been electrified some years before. With the extension of the overhead, there was a need for machines that could get along at a good pace without doing either themselves or the track any damage. The EW's fitted the bill admirably. They hauled heavy suburban trains with ease, achieving almost multiple unit style acceleration away from stops, and they managed heavy goods trains with the same aplomb.

The seven-locomotive fleet was not, however, used to its full capacity as in the 1960s diesel locomotives took over most goods workings, although EW's were sometimes used as bankers on the climb to Pukerua Bay. Their other main job — peak-hour suburban carriage trains used to augment the multiple unit service — vanished in 1982 when a big fleet of new multiple units arrived from Hungary. From then on, all peak services could be covered by multiple units and the EW fleet quietly vanished into storage, into the scrapyard and into preservation. Given different circumstances, there is no doubt that these popular and efficient machines could have worked out a full 40 years.

One EW has been preserved by New Zealand Rail. There is another at the Ferrymead Railway, Christchurch.
Specifications
Wheel arrangement: Bo—Bo—Bo
Weight: 75 tons (76 tonnes)
Traction motors: 6
Power output: 1800 hp (1342 kW)
Tractive effort: 23,400 lbs (104 kN)
Wheel diam.: 36.5 in (927 mm)   Length: 62 feet (18.897 metres)

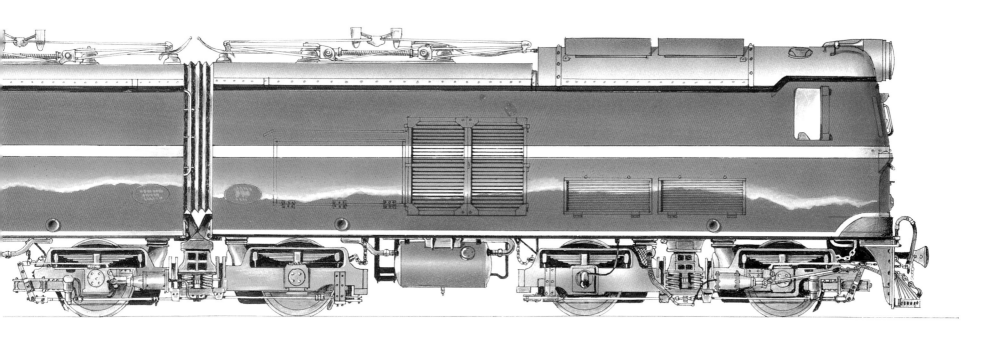

Class DF — 1954

New Zealand's first main line diesel-electric locomotives, the 10 DF class, represented something of a blind street in the history of NZR motive power development, yet they are significant not only because they were the first of their type but also because they demonstrated the advantages of this form of traction over steam. Originally it was announced that 31 big main line locomotives would be ordered from English Electric in Britain but the order was amended — there would be 10 of the big ones plus 21 smaller ones. The big ones, the DF's, would be 1500 hp (1118 kW) with a cab at each end; the others would be single-ended and of half that power (class DG). Railways demanded that the axle load of the DF must not exceed 12 tonnes so the makers adopted the wheel arrangement of 2-Co+Co-2 — two two-axle unpowered bogies at the outer ends and two inner three-axle bogies each with all axles powered.

Heavy and cumbersome though they were, the DF's, when placed in service on the North Island Main Trunk, showed they could haul more than the eight-coupled steam locomotives and save several hours on the run. Their electrical equipment was excellent, but there were problems with the diesel engines so, when the DA class arrived (developing almost as much power but weighing some 30 tonnes less), the DF's were consigned to less important routes, in particular the Bay of Plenty. In the bay, they settled down to do some steady work on the light rail still in place on that line, but they continued to require a relatively high level of maintenance. This, coupled with the fact that they comprised a numerically small class, led to their withdrawal by 1975, by which time some of the class had hardly

been in service for 20 years. NZR, meanwhile, had decided that the United States was the place to shop for the sort of locomotives best suited to New Zealand conditions.

The DF and its small DG relative were designed in the classic cab unit style developed in the United States before World War II and were, in their own way, quite handsome machines.

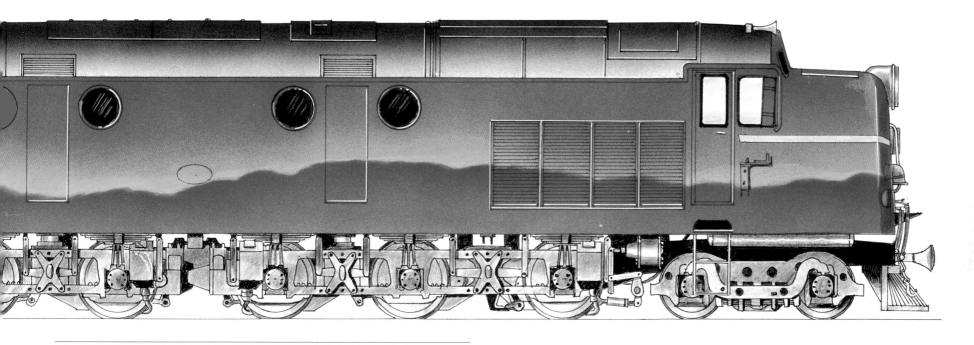

One DF is preserved, at Pacific Metal Industries, Otahuhu.

Specifications

Wheel arrangement: 2−Co+Co−2
Weight: 108 tons (110 tonnes)
Diesel engine output: 1500 hp (1119 kW)
Traction motors: 6
Tractive effort: 28,000 lbs (124 kN)
Diam. of driving wheels: 37 in (940 mm)   Length: 61 feet 3 inches (18.669 metres)

Class DG — 1955

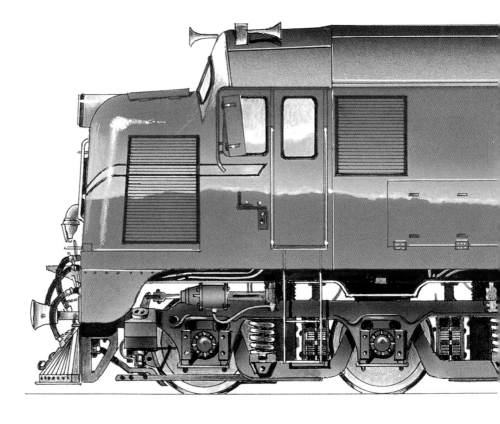

This locomotive was the 'half DF' referred to earlier. Unlike the DF, with its cab at both ends, the DG was a single-ended design, but very much a member of the same 'family' as the bigger machine. Whereas the DF had a 12-cylinder diesel engine, the DG had a 6-cylinder type, and was heavy in relation to its power output, scaling in at some 70 tonnes. Eleven of the 42 DG's were sent to the South Island on arrival and as they were to work only on the heavy-rail South Island Main Trunk their suspension was altered to place more weight on the powered axles. These were classified DH, although in later years they were altered back to DG configuration. The North Island locomotives worked on most provincial lines, although their power output meant that they were often seen working in multiple, coupled back to back. By 1976 all the North Island DG's had been transferred south, displaced by more powerful locomotives. They plodded on for a few more years until 1978 when 10 were rebuilt with new cabs somewhat along the lines of those fitted to DC locomotives, the aim being to provide better working conditions for the crews. The unaltered locomotives were scrapped when heavy repairs became necessary.

In both the DG and the DF the driver sat in the middle of the cab, with his assistant on the left. The original idea was that these machines would be single manned, but this did not come about until both DF's and DG's had long departed from the scene. In spite of the alterations, the recabbed machines lasted only a few more years, all having being withdrawn by the end of 1983. Thus the short era of the classic cab unit diesel came to an end.

Three DG's are preserved at the Weka Pass Railway, Waipara and one by the Diesel Traction Group, Ferrymead, Christchurch.
Specifications
Wheel arrangement: A1A–A1A
Weight: 68.9 tons (70 tonnes)
Diesel engine output: 750 hp (559 kW)
Traction motors: 4
Tractive effort: 20,200 lbs (90 kN)
Diam. of driving wheels: 37 in (940 mm)   Length: 45 feet (13.716 metres)

Class DA — 1955

The beginning of the present era of diesel traction on New Zealand Railways can be traced back to 1955 when 30 G-12 standard locomotives were ordered from General Motors, the first bought from the United States since the Baldwin Aa of 1915. At 12 ft (3.7 m) high and 9 ft (2.3 m) wide, these locomotives were well outside the loading gauge set in the Vogel era so considerable effort had to be put into lowering tunnel floors, widening loco shed doors and so on. In fact, about the only concession made to the NZR loading gauge had been to curve the top corner of the cab roof.

The DA's went into service on North Island lines, at first the Main Trunk and later on most provincial routes, and quickly proved to be reliable, economical and powerful. Within months, 10 more were ordered from Clyde, Australia and over the next few years more came from GM, Canada, so that ultimately 146 were in service, to become NZR's largest-ever locomotive class. The DA's proved satisfactory on passenger trains even if their maximum speed of around 60 mph (100 km/h) was below that of the steam locos they replaced; they were excellent freight locomotives capable of hauling 2000-tonne trains on easy grades, and hard slogging work in the hills. They not only succeeded in finishing off North Island steam traction for good but also set the pattern for future motive power developments.

The illustration shows a DA's in the livery adopted as standard in 1976. Before this the locomotives were painted red with silver flashes, the same colour scheme as for the articulated railcar. The class was more or less extinct by the end of the 1980s, but 85 received a new lease of life when they were rebuilt.

(Known as Class DC, these machines will be dealt with shortly.)

The DA legacy has another aspect. Because these locomotives were overgauge, NZR had to begin enlarging clearances. When the ISO container arrived on the scene in the late 1960s the task of fitting the system to handle these was easier because of the work already carried out for the DA's.

DA locomotives are preserved at Motat, Auckland; the Main Line Steam Trust (2); Steam Incorporated, Paekakariki (2); and by New Zealand Rail.

Specifications

Wheel arrangement: A1A−A1A

Weight: 76 tons (77 tonnes)

Diesel engine output: 1425 hp (1063 kW)

Traction motors: 4

Tractive effort: 28,000 lbs (124 kN)

Diam. of driving wheels: 40 in (1016 mm) Length: 46 feet 3 inches (14.097 metres)

Twin-Unit Railcars — 1955

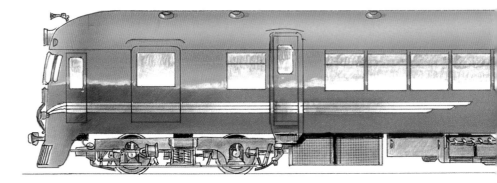

These were the best and the worst of railcars. They worked on virtually every passenger route and dominated most of those routes for almost two decades. Fast and comfortable, they were the first rail vehicles to offer reclining seats for second-class passengers. They had ample toilet facilities and luggage space, even a separate compartment for the guard. But they also suffered innumerable mechanical failures, costing a small fortune to keep on the road. They were designed by Drewry and built by the Birmingham Carriage and Wagon Company. Thirty-five entered service, powered by underfloor Fiat diesel engines, one under each section of the articulated set. Each car could carry 88 passengers and they could run in multiples of up to three. But there were perpetual mechanical problems, and fitters frequently laboured on into the night to have a car ready for the next day's service.

Nevertheless, in 1968 three were converted for use on a luxury businessman's service between Hamilton and Auckland, fitted out with carpets and other on-board refinements including a small staffed kitchen. Painted in a unique blue livery, the cars failed to attract economic loads on this run so they were switched to a new daytime Wellington-Auckland run which proved so successful that, a few years later, brand-new cars were ordered to take over from them. In this guise the service became known as the Blue Streak — a rare example of a railwayman's nickname becoming official. When the new Main Trunk Silver Fern railcars entered service in 1972 the Blue Streaks went on to the New Plymouth run where they lasted until 1977.

The rest of the railcars were withdrawn by 1979, although 14 had a brief second career as locomotive-hauled carriages. Painted green, these cars carried the nickname 'grass grubs'; all had gone by 1985. Sadly, no examples of this largest class of railcar were preserved. The illustrations show both the standard and the special Blue Streak liveries.

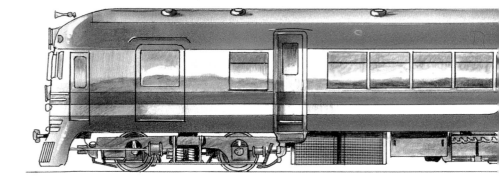

None of the twin-unit railcars survived to be preserved.
Specifications
Engines (no., power): 2, 209 hp each (156 kW)
Transmission: Diesel mechanical
Weight: 52.9 tons (53.7 tonnes)
Seats: 88   Length: 107 feet (32.614 metres)

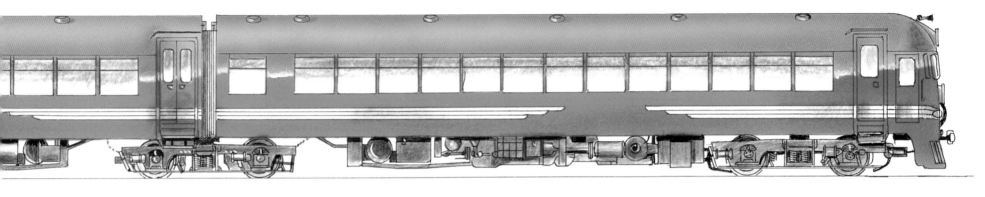

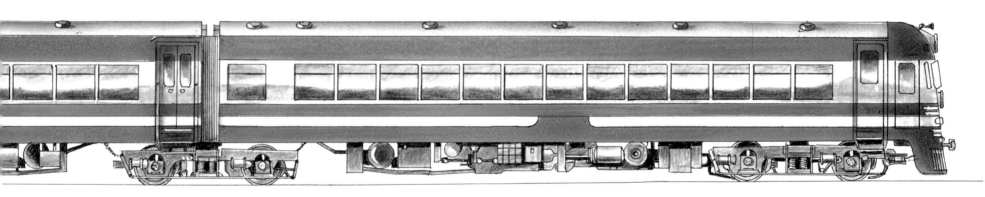

Class DSC — 1959

Only by riding one of the rigid wheelbase 0-6-0 shunting locomotives around a marshalling yard could the layman appreciate just how rough-riding these little machines were, rough for the driver and his mate, and especially rough for the shunter standing on the front step. So there would have been sighs of relief in 1959 when the first of a new double bogie diesel-electric shunting loco entered service. These were real Rolls-Royce machines compared with the 0-6-0s, and literally so as far as the first 18 were concerned since these products of the British Thomson-Houston Company of England were powered by Rolls-Royce diesel engines, one under each hood. Of course these machines were not designed primarily for a soft ride; they were bought to work in the largest marshalling yards, where increasing train weights left the smaller locos rather out of breath.

Subsequent batches of DSC's came from NZR's Hillside and Addington workshops, boosting the fleet to a total of 70 machines. The New Zealand-made DSC's were powered by Leyland engines; in later years the DSC's wore out their original power units so new ones were installed. With their large cabs and excellent visibility, these have been popular locos, and their 40 mph (64 km/h) top speed has also seen them work on short main line shunting jobs. Recent years, however, have seen some scrappings as the heaviest shunting work has been taken over by the more powerful DSG class.

No DSC's have yet been preserved.
Specifications
Wheel arrangement: Bo—Bo
Weight: 40.5 tons (41 tonnes)
Diesel engine output: 420 hp (313 kW)
Traction motors: 4
Tractive effort: 10,300 lbs (46 kN)
Diam. of driving wheels: 37 in (940 mm) Length: 37 feet 10 inches (11.659 metres)

2000

Class DI — 1966

With the DA class firmly establised on main North Island routes, in the mid-1960s NZR went shopping for a lighter medium-powered machine for secondary lines. As it was, two new classes answering this description were placed in serice — 17 DB class 705 kW locomotives for General Motors (a lighter and less powerful version of the DA) and five 755 kW Co-Co machines from English Electric's Rocklea, Queensland plant, which became Class DI.

The DI is historically important as it was the first on NZR to have the Co-Co wheel arrangement, in other words two three-axle bogies, each with its own traction motor. Unlike the DA, the DB and the DG, the DI had all its weight available for traction, and set the standard for today's generation of diesel-electric main line machines, the DX and the DF.

The DI's were intended for North Island secondary lines but a few of the five worked in the south initially before joining others in the class on working the lightly laid but heavily trafficked Hamilton-Paeroa-Tauranga line. With the opening of the Kaimai Tunnel in 1978, the old line via Paeroa through to Waihi was closed and the DI's went south again, to be based in Dunedin. They ended their lives shunting in Napier and Wellington, the last being withdrawn in 1988—89. No doubt their end was hastened because they were numerically a small class, and because their design did not suit them for one-person operation.

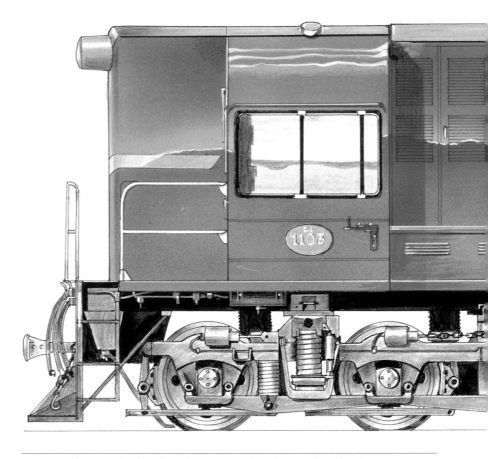

A preserved DI can be found at the Ferrymead Railway, Christchurch.
Specifications
Wheel arrangement: Co—Co
Weight: 60 tons (61 tonnes)
Diesel engine output: 1012 hp (755 kW)
Traction motors: 6
Tractive effort: 29, 686 lbs (132 kN)
Diam. of driving wheels: 36.6 in (940 mm)
Length: 45 feet 3 inches (13.792 metres)

Class DJ — 1968

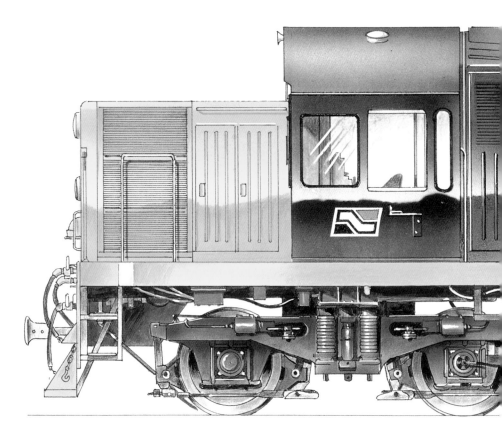

With the DA locomotives firmly in control on North Island lines, NZR engineers turned to the South Island in the mid-1960s and drew up specifications for a light axle load medium-powered locomotive which could run not only on the South Island Main Trunk line but also on the lighter track of secondary and branch lines. The successful tenderer was Mitsubishi Heavy Industries of Japan, who supplied 64 triple bogie locomotives which became Class DJ. The DJ's bogie arrangement was designed to produce minimum wheel flange wear on sharp curves and also to spread the weight. The locomotives were powered by Caterpillar engines linked to an ac/dc transmission with solid state rectifiers to convert the ac to dc for the traction motors — the first use of this modern system on NZR. The triple bogie arrangement would also be used on the North Island Main Trunk electric locomotives in 1987.

The DJ's dominated the South Island for years; they enabled the last of the steam locomotives to be withdrawn from service and were to be found on all parts of the system. Initial problems with engine overheating meant the engines were derated for some time but modifications more or less solved this problem. The transfer of DC and DX locomotives from the North Island after the Main Trunk electrification meant that scrapping of the DJ's gained momentum. Some had gone by the early 1980s, and today the class is virtually extinct. At the time of writing, however, nine were in store at Hutt workshops awaiting a buyer and another five were set aside for working the Otago Excursion Train Trust's Taieri Gorge excursion train out of Dunedin.

DJ's were originally painted in a rather pink shade of red, later replaced by bright red. Some were painted in a unique blue livery to match the Southerner express, but in latter years all were painted in a blue version of the standard livery, as seen in the illustration. Their strengths and weaknesses aside, the DJ's would not have been suitable for single manning owing to the height of the short hood in front of the cab, so their demise was inevitable.

Several DJ's have been acquired by the Otago Excursion Train Trust, Dunedin; there is one at Ranfurly.

Specifications
Wheel arrangement: Bo−Bo−Bo
Weight: 63 tons (64 tonnes)
Diesel engine output: 901 hp (672 kW)
Traction motors: 6
Tractive effort: 28,786 lbs (128 kN)
Diam. of driving wheels: 37 in (940 mm)   Length: 45 feet 9 inches (14.097 metres)

Class EO (formerly EA) – 1968

Since 1923 the EO class electric locomotives had toiled up the 1 in 33 grade from Otira through the tunnel to Arthur's Pass, but after more than 40 years' service they were, if not worn out, then certainly obsolete. NZR went to Toshiba of Japan for their replacements — five new Bo-Bos, of similar weight and size to their predecessors, but, reflecting technological progress over more than four decades, almost twice as powerful.

The new machines were fitted with a cab at one end and, like the EO's had end access doors, important for a locomotive intended to spend much of its working life in a tunnel where side door access only could bring problems in an emergency.

Like the EO's, the new EA's, as they were initially classified, worked in threes using multiple unit control, but their capacity was much greater — a triple unit could haul 620 tonnes up the grade compared with the 375-tonne maximum load for three EO's.

In recent years, the five machines, which were reclassified EO about 1979, have been assisted on heavy export coal trains by leaving the diesel-electrics on for the run up the hill, and the time may yet come when more use has to be made of diesel power; experiments have shown that ventilation problems can be overcome. Meanwhile the present EOs seem certain to remain in service for as long as their predecessors did.

None is preserved as all five remain in service.
Specifications
Wheel arrangement: Bo−Bo
Weight: 54 tons (54.9 tonnes)
Traction motors: 4
Power output: 1286 np (960 kW)
Tractive effort: 22, 713 pounds (101 kN)
Diam. of driving wheels: 39.6 in (1016 mm)
Length: 37 feet 7 inches (11.582 metres)

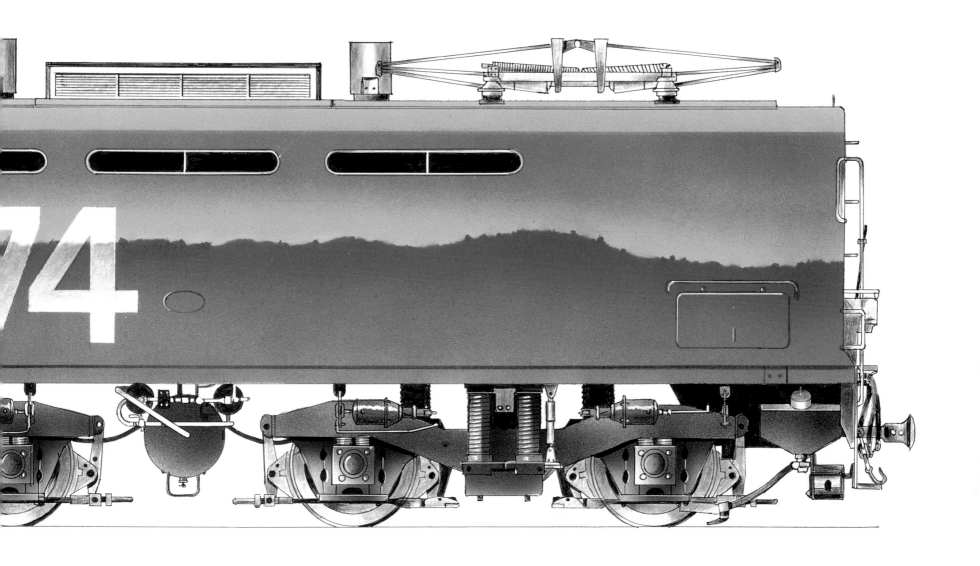

Class DX — 1972

The air-conditioned all-sleeper Silver Star Express placed in service on the Auckland-Wellington run in 1971 was one of the prime tasks for which the DX class was intended. Built by General Electric in the United States, these big machines were each almost twice as powerful as a DA class and also faster, being designed to run at 75 mph (120 km/h). Unlike the DA, the DX has ac/dc transmission and in this and other areas represents a second generation of main line diesel power on NZR. There were 15 DX's in the first order, and a second order of 34 was delivered from 1975. Initially the class worked on the North Island Main Trunk but as more arrived they also took over the heaviest jobs on other lines. Main Trunk express and express goods trains were their forte until the central section of the route was electrified. Some of those displaced by electrification were sent to the South Island so, at the time of writing, many long-distance passenger and goods trains in both islands are DX-powered.

As this book goes to press, a DX is in the process of being rebuilt as described on page 60.

When it went into service the DX was NZR's most powerful locomotive up to that time, a position it lost when the North Island Main Trunk electric locomotives entered service.

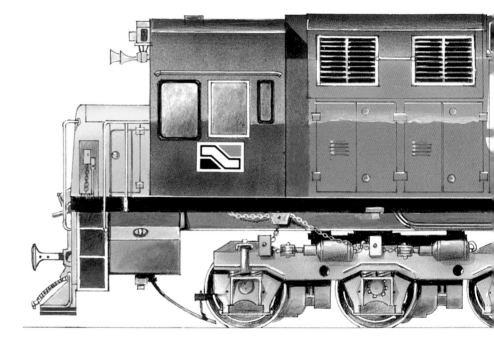

All DX's remain in service.
Specifications
Wheel arrangement: Co—Co
Weight: 96 tons (97.5 tonnes)
Diesel engine output: 2749 hp (2050 kW)
Traction motors: 6
Tractive effort: 46,552 lbs (207 kN)
Diam. of driving wheels: 37 in (940 mm)   Length: 58 feet 3 inches (17.945 metres)

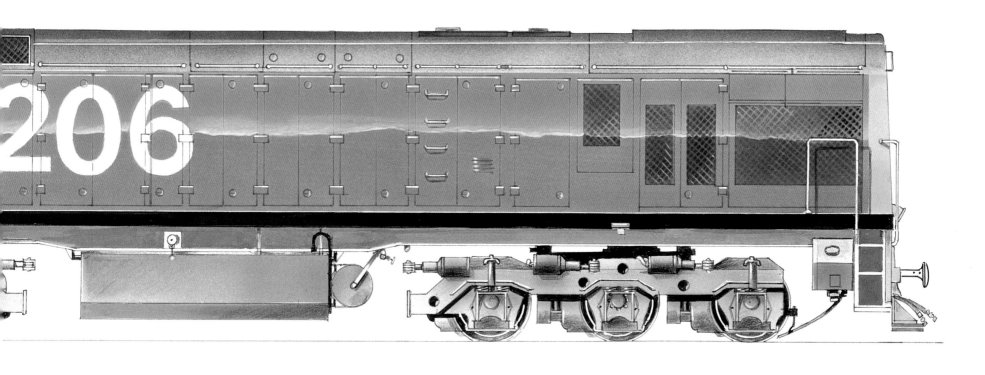

Class RM — 1972

All NZR's many and varied railcars have been RMs, but today only one type is in service, comprising the three Silver Fern machines. These big twin-unit diesel-electric railcars were built by the Nissho-Iwai Company of Japan in 1972 for the Auckland-Wellington daytime service, which, as has been mentioned, was inaugurated by refurbished articulated Fiat 88-seat railcars in 1968. The Silver Ferns are 47.4 m long, 3.79 m high and 2.74 m wide, big by NZR standards, and seat 96 passengers in reclining seats. They are air-conditioned, and have a small kitchen area from which refreshments are served.

Each is powered by a Caterpillar diesel engine of 755 kW with a separate small unit for auxiliary power, both engines being installed in an above-floor compartment at the end of one car, this end being carried on a six-wheeled bogie of which two axles are powered. The outer bogie at the end of the other car is also fitted with traction motors. The Ferns are capable of 75 mph (120 km/h) officially but have been recorded at speeds a good deal higher. The cars are sheathed in unpainted stainless steel, which gives them a sleek modern look from the side, but their appearance is rather marred by uncompromisingly flat ends.

The railcars ran the Auckland-Wellington daytime service satisfactorily for many years, proving popular with passengers. In late 1991 they were switched to new routes from Auckland to Rotorua and Tauranga where they are again proving to be effective generators of passenger traffic. Their successors on the Trunk are carriage trains, fitted with observation cars and generally hauled by DX locomotives.

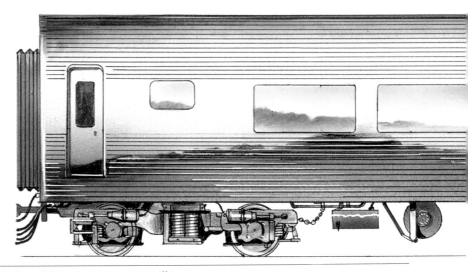

All three Silver Fern RM's are still in service.
Specifications
Engines (no., power): 1, 898.5 hp (670 kW)
Transmission: Diesel electric
Weight: 109.25 tons (111 tonnes)
Seats: 96   Length: 154 feet 2 inches (47.440 metres)

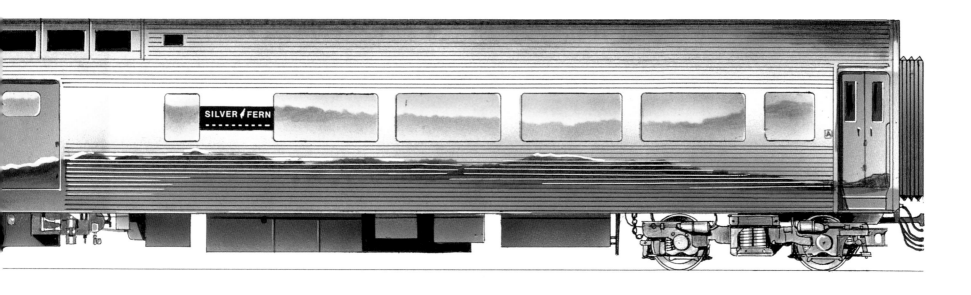

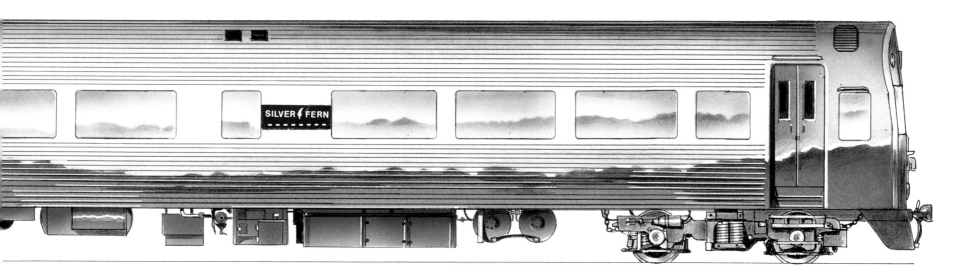

Class DC — 1978

More than a second glance is necessary to ascertain that this illustration shows a rebuilt DA. The new cab and low short hood, giving far better working conditions for the crew, is obvious; what is not obvious is that the DC has a more powerful diesel engine (1230 kW as opposed to 1060 kW) plus newer and more modern control gear, with all other components, large and small, thoroughly overhauled. The work was started in 1978, all but five of the 85 conversions being done by Clyde Engineering, Australia. The other five were rebuilt at NZR's Hutt workshops. The result is a fleet of locomotives virtually renewed, and ready to run until the turn of the century.

Initially, like their DA ancestors, the DC's were confined to the North Island, but about a third of the fleet has more recently been shipped south where they do such jobs as the Midland line coal trains. The DA's chosen for conversion to DC were all from the Canadian-built batches which went into service from 1961 to 1967.

All DCs remain in service.
Specifications
Wheel arrangement: A1A–A1A
Weight: 80.7 tons (82 tonnes)
Diesel engine output: 1649 hp (1230 kW)
Traction motors: 4
Tractive effort: 31,484 lbs (140 kN)
Diam. of driving wheels: 40 in (1016 mm)   Length: 45 feet 9 inches (14.097 metres)

Class TR — 1939, 1978

This record of New Zealand railway motive power would be incomplete without reference to the TR class of shunting tractor. These little machines of various makes, but generally of around 20 tonnes in weight and 140 kW in power output, had their origins in 1924 when NZR bought a little four-wheeled machine from the American Adamson Motor Company comprising, in essence, a standard Fordson farm tractor on railway wheels — literally a shunting tractor.

The Adamson-Fordson was a mixed success. It was tried out at a variety of depots and yards and although the idea was sound it was not quite what was wanted. After another couple of efforts, NZR got it right in 1936 when it put into service the first of a batch of 0-4-0 70 hp shunters from Drewry of Britain. These were proper little locomotives, but they were still classed as tractors because it was intended that they should be worked by station yard staff and not by engine drivers, since their use would only be intermittent. In any case, they were far smaller and simpler than 'proper' locomotives, and engine drivers were paid more than traffic staff.

The first batch of Drewrys was followed, in 1939, by a batch of 0-6-0 s, but later machines reverted to 0-4-0, from makers including Bagnall, A. and G. Price and Hitachi.

The prime role of these machines was to shunt wagons around medium-sized station yards — yards too small to warrant a 'proper' shunting locomotive with its own full-time crew, and yet too large to be conveniently shunted by main line trains. The tractors were used to place wagons for loading and unloading in goods sheds and at stockyard races, and they also gathered up all the wagons destined for each passing main line train so that through services were not delayed.

The last of the TR's to enter service were the only ones of the class to be built by NZR, and it is one of these nine machines which is illustrated here. They were built at Hillside railway workshops between 1973 and 1978 and are powered by Gardner diesel engines driving through torque converters. Although the TR fleet has shrunk in recent years, they are still to be found in many medium-sized railway yards and also working for private industry.

Preserved TR of various makes can be found at the Bush Tramway Club, Rotowaro; Pleasant Point Railway; MOTAT, Auckland; Ferrymead Railway; Glenbrook Vintage Railway, Oamaru Steam and Rail; Plains Railway, Ashburton; Khandallah Park, Wellington; Founders Park, Nelson; Ocean Beach Railway, Dunedin; and Main Trunk Rail, Ohakune.

Specifications
Wheel arrangement: 0-4-0
Weight: 20.4 tonnes
Power output: 112 kW
Tractive effort: 34 kN
Diam. of driving wheels: 1010 mm
Length: 22 feet 11 inches (6.991 metres)

Class DF — 1979

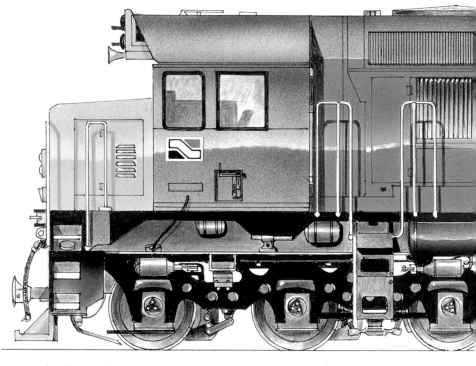

The DF locomotives, the latest additions to New Zealand Rail's main line diesel-electric fleet, were designed very much as freight locomotives, and could be described as a modern version of the DA or DC, with a similar horsepower, but with six traction motors. As a result, their tractive effort is higher than the DC — 205 kN compared with the DC's 145 kN — and is quite close to that of the DX, which develops 239 kN. The DF's come from the same stable as the DA — General Motors in the United States — and, as can be seen from the illustration, look rather like a DC, which is, of course, a DA rebuild. Needless to say, the DF has all the modern features, including ac/dc drive.

In service the DF's have proved very successful freight locomotives, initially working on North Island lines and now in both islands. They have dominated services in South Auckland/Bay of Plenty as well as on the Christchurch-Picton line, and have also seen service on many other routes. In spite of their tender years, however, they have become somewhat out of date in that the need today is not for low-speed plodders but for locomotives with sufficient power to run fast with the same weight of train. This is in response to continuing customer demand for shorter transit times. Accordingly, in 1992 a DF was fitted with a turbo blower and other modifications, which increase the engine horsepower by 50 per cent. Approval has been obtained to convert another 10 locomotives and it is expected that the rest of the fleet will be modified too, allowing DF's to do what they do now — haul heavy goods trains, but at express goods train speeds.

The modified machine has been reclassified DFT and is distinguished by a hump on the top of the long hood, necessary to house the new exhaust system fitted in connection with the installation of the exhaust-gas-driven turbo blower. When New Zealand Rail does go shopping for new main line motive power (and there is no immediate need at the time of writing) what may be acquired could be rather like the DFT — a medium-powered six traction motor turbo-charged locomotive with all the latest features such as sophisticated wheel slip control systems. Time will tell.

All DF's remain in service.
Specifications
Wheel arrangement: Co–Co
Weight: 84.5 tons (85.9 tonnes)
Diesel engine output: 1649.5 hp (1230 kW)
Traction motors: 6
Tractive effort: 44,528 lbs (198 kN)
Diam. of driving wheels: 37 in (940 mm)   Length: 54 feet 2 inches (16.688 metres)

Class DSG — 1981

By the end of the 1970s trains were getting heavier — 2000 tonnes was not uncommon in some areas — and there was a need for even more powerful shunting locomotives. Mitsui of Japan was contracted to supply the first of what was to become a 24-unit fleet of DSGs. Like the earlier DSC, the DSG is a double bogie twin-engined diesel-electric with centre cab. The DSG develops 160 kN of tractive effort, well above the DSC's 100 kN, and works today in the busiest yards, displacing DSC's from these tasks. The DSG was made to the maximum possible dimensions as far as height and width of the cab is concerned, ensuring the best possible lookout for the driver. It is a tribute to the NZR engineers who prepared the specifications that the DSG is a most popular machine with those who work it.

Five further locomotives were built to the same basic design, this time with only one engine each. The first was imported and the other four were built at Addington workshops. At low speeds the DSJ, as it is known, is virtually equal to a twin-engined DSG.

All DSG's remain in service.
Specifications
Wheel arrangement: Bo–Bo
Weight: 55 tons (56 tonnes)
Diesel engine output: 2, total 940 hp (700 kW)
Traction motors: 4
Tractive effort: 29,236 lbs (130 kN)
Diam. of driving wheels: 37 in (940 mm)   Length: 43 feet 9 inches (13.490 metres)

Class EM/ET — 1981

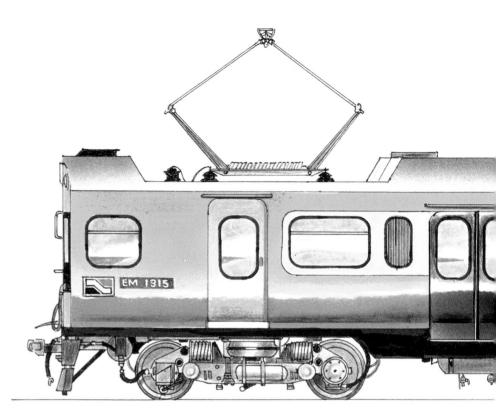

Apart from the Silver Fern railcars, the only post-war designs of passenger rolling stock on NZR are the EM and ET class electric multiple unit carriages running on the Wellington 1500V dc suburban system. A total of 44 two-car sets (each of one EM motor coach and one ET trailer coach) was built by the Hungarian firm of Ganz Mavag, the first reaching New Zealand at the end of 1981. Their entry into service allowed for the retirement of the earliest English Electric units, which had passed the 40-year mark, and for the withdrawal of the locomotive-hauled carriage trains that had been used at peak times to supplement the multiple units. The new cars are wider, higher and longer than their predecessors, have better seats and lighting and also ride on air suspension, giving a far smoother ride. A two-car set seats 148, compared with 128 in a corresponding English Electric set, and up to four two-car sets can be run in multiple.

These vehicles look very much like British or European trains of the 1970s — they are painted in a unique olive green and cream livery with yellow ends. They seem destined to be the mainstay of the capital's electric train service well into the 21st century.

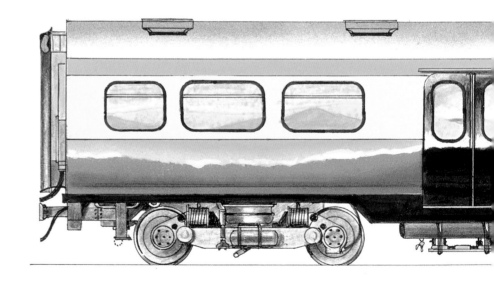

All EM's and ET's remain in service.
Specifications
Traction motors (no., power): 4, 536.4 hp total (400 kW)
Weight: EM, 36.6 tons (37.2 tonnes); ET, 33.3 tons (33.8 tonnes)
Seats: EM, 70 ET, 78   Length: 70 feet (21.530 metres)

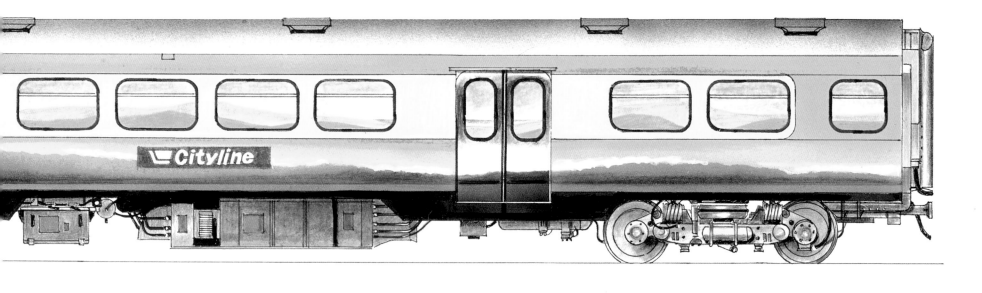

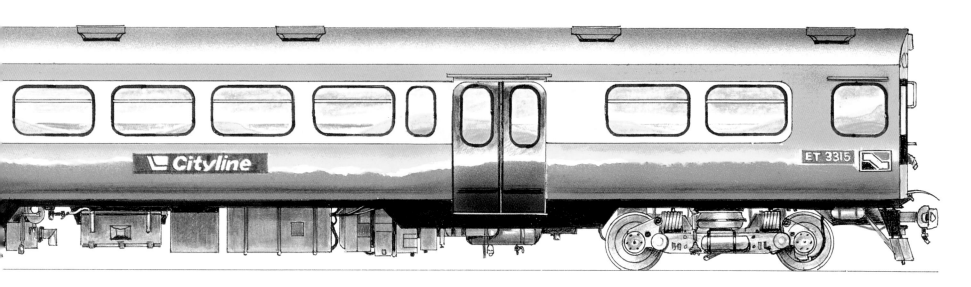

Class 30 (EF) — 1987

Electrification of the North Island Main Trunk was recommended by a 1950 NZR report but, for various reasons, it was decided to replace steam traction with diesel-electrics. Thirty years on another proposal was approved and in 1983 tenders were accepted for electrifying the Hamilton-Palmerston North section (410 km) at 25 kV ac, the work including the improvement of clearances, easing of some curves, erection of overhead and the supply of 22 Bo-Bo-Bo 3000 kW locomotives from Brush Electrical Machines of Britain. Known as the Class 30s, and more recently as EFs, these locomotives are by far the most powerful to run on NZR, with the ability to start a 1000-tonne train on a 1 in 50 gradient. They incorporate many modern features including regenerative braking, thyristor control, fault annunciators, event monitor and so on.

With their entry into service, operating costs on the electrified section have been reduced through running heavier trains at higher speeds; the EFs are normally used only for goods trains as it has been found more efficient for the diesel locomotives on both the day and night Wellington-Auckland trains to run through without stopping for locomotive changes at Palmerston North and Hamilton. The class has had its share of teething problems but the soundness of the basic design is apparent from the fact that the Channel Tunnel locomotives will run on triple bogies based on those developed for the EF.

The class entered commercial service about March 1988 and the whole electrification project was officially opened in June that year. The book life of the project is 40 years, so the EFs should be around for a long time to come.

All Class 30s remain in service.
Specifications
Wheel arrangement: Bo–Bo–Bo
Weight: 106.3 tons (108 tonnes)
Traction motors: 6
Power output: 4023 hp (3000 kW)
Tractive effort: 67,467 lbs (300 kN)
Wheel diam.: 43.3 in (1100 mm)   Length: 63 feet 8 inches (19.610 metres)

Class DXR — 1993

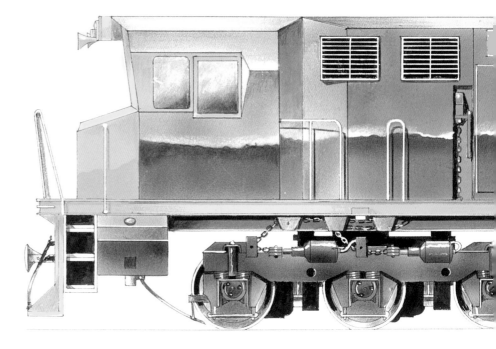

J ust as this book was off to the printer a new face was appearing on the New Zealand railway scene — a rebuilt DX class diesel electric locomotive, upgraded to 3200 hp, and the nation's most powerful diesel.

As already noted, the DX class entered service from 1972; 20 years on these 2750 hp (2050 kW) machines were due for a complete overhaul. Over those 20 years developments in locomotive engineering had left the DX somewhat out of date so the decision had to be made whether to rebuild or upgrade. Rebuilding would result in a 'new' 20-year-old locomotive, whereas upgrading would see a number of modern improvements built into the locomotive, resulting in more power and improved reliability.

The latter course was chosen and in the second half of 1993 the first DX rebuild, now classed DXR, emerged from New Zealand Rail's Hutt workshops. As can be seen from the illustration, the appearance of the DXR is markedly different from the DX shown on page 44. The new cab, unlike the old, is specifically designed for single-person crewing, and the short hood has been rebuilt to allow for a walkway across the front of the locomotive; other changes to the superstructure will also be noted.

The diesel engine has been fitted with new cylinder heads, liners, pistons and connecting rods, and cooling, lubrication and fuel systems upgraded to match the increased power putput. New traction motors are fitted plus a new gear set which will reduce the locomotives maximum possible speed by 5 kmh but this should not affect in-service train speeds and yet give a worthwhile increase in pulling power. The axle load rises from 16.5 to 17.5 tonnes as additional adhesive weight is necessary if the additional power is to be fully used.

After the DXR has run its trials a decision will be made on whether to upgrade the whole fleet. With the sale of New Zealand Rail to private enterprise, this decision will no doubt be an early priority for the new owners. Suffice to say that the railway has been well served by its motive power engineers for more than a century, and that the new owners will take over not only a locomotive fleet in fine fettle, but also one with an upgrading programme already under way. The drawing shows the locomotive in New Zealand Rail's current blue livery-details of the actual colour scheme to be used had not been

finalised when this book was completed.

Specifications
As for the DX except for power and weight as outlined above. Precise figures unavailable as the locomotive was not completed at press time.

New Zealand Rail's Locomotive Fleet

The following lists show main line and shunting locomotives in service on New Zealand's railway network as at 1990. The list does not include the small TR class machines which are not classed as locomotives, and nor does it include diesel or electric multiple unit stock.

These lists were extracted with permission from *NZR Locomotives and Railcars 1990*, by T.A. McGavin, published by the New Zealand Railway and Locomotive Society, P.O. Box 5134, Wellington. Readers wanting more detailed information are referred to this publication.

Diesel electric shunting locomotives

Class DSC Bo-Bo
Total: 50

Road TMS	numbers Pre-TMS	Maker's numbers	Date in service
British-Thomson-Houston			
DSC2026	402	1067	5/1959
DSC2067	406	1071	7/1959
DSC2191	417	1082	11/1959
NZR (Addington)			
DSC2203	418	398	10/1962
DSC2216	419	399	12/1962
DSC2229	420	400	3/1963
DSC2244	422	402	5/1963
DSC2257	423	403	7/1963
DSC2285	425	405	9/1963
DSC2298	426	406	11/1963
DSC2312	427	407	11/1963
NZR (Hillside)			
DSC2325	428	408	11/1962
DSC2338	429	409	2/1963
DSC2340	430	410	3/1963
DSC2353	431	411	5/1963
DSC2366	432	412	6/1963
DSC2379	433	413	7/1963
DSC2381	434	414	9/1963
DSC2394	435	415	10/1963
DSC2406	436	416	12/1963
DSC2419	437	417	3/1964
NZR (Addington)			
DSC2421	438	418	11/1964
DSC2434	439	419	12/1964
DSC2447	440	420	2/1965
DSC2462	441	421	3/1965
DSC2475	442	422	5/1965
DSC2488	443	423	8/1965
NZR (Hillside)			
DSC2490	444	424	12/1964
DSC2502	445	425	12/1964
DSC2515	446	426	3/1965
DSC2528	447	427	3/1965
DSC2530	448	428	6/1965
DSC2543	449	429	8/1965
NZR (Addington)			
DSC2556	450	430	9/1966
DSC2569	451	431	12/1966
DSC2571	452	432	12/1966
DSC2584	453	433	12/1966
DSC2597	454	434	2/1967
DSC2609	455	435	3/1967
DSC2611	456	436	5/1967
DSC2624	457	437	6/1967
DSC2637	458	438	8/1967
DSC2652	459	439	9/1967
NZR (Hillside)			
DSC2665	460	440	9/1966
DSC2678	461	441	10/1966
DSC2680	462	442	12/1966
DSC2693	463	443	12/1966
DSC2705	464	444	6/1967
DSC2718	465	445	7/1967
DSC2720	466	446	9/1967
DSC2733	467	447	10/1967
DSC2746	468	448	11/1967
DSC2759	469	449	12/1967

Class DH Bo-Bo
Total: 6

Road TMS	numbers Pre-TMS	Maker's numbers	Date in service
General Electric USA			
DH2816	900	41766	5/1979
DH2822	901	41767	11/1978
DH2839	902	41768	12/1978
DH2845	903	41769	9/1978
DH2851	904	41770	11/1978
DH2868	905	41771	3/1979

Class DSG Bo-Bo
Total: 24

Road TMS	numbers Pre-TMS	Maker's numbers	Date in service
Toshiba, Japan			
DSG3005	—	5601061-1	3/1981
DSG3018	—	5601061-2	3/1981
DSG3020	—	5601061-3	3/1981
DSG3033	—	5601061-4	3/1981
DSG3046	—	5601061-5	3/1981
DSG3059	—	5601061-6	3/1981
DSG3061	—	5601177-1	3/1982
DSG3074	—	5601177-2	3/1982
DSG3087	—	5601177-3	3/1982
DSG3101	—	5601177-4	3/1982
DSG3114	—	5601177-5	3/1982
DSG3127	—	5601177-6	3/1982
DSG3155	—	5601201-1	6/1982
DSG3168	—	5601201-2	6/1982
DSG3170	—	5601201-3	6/1982
DSG3196	—	5601201-4	6/1982
DSG3208	—	5601201-5	6/1982
DSG3210	—	5601201-6	6/1982
DSG3236	—	5601342-1	10/1983
DSG3249	—	5601342-2	10/1983
DSG3251	—	5601342-3	10/1983
DSG3264	—	5601342-4	10/1983
DSG3277	—	5601342-5	10/1983
DSG3304	—	5601342-6	10/1983

Class DSJ Bo-Bo
Total: 5

Road numbers	Maker's numbers	Date in service
Toshiba, Japan		
DSJ4004	5601342-7	3/1984
NZR (Addington)		
DSJ4017		12/1984
DSJ4032		
DSJ4045		
DSJ4060		

Mainline diesel-electric locomotives

Class DC A1A-A1A
Total: 85

Road TMS	numbers Pre-TMS	Maker's numbers	Date in service
Clyde Engineering, South Australia			
DC4006	1551	78/866	3/1978
DC4012	1552	78/867	3/1978
DC4029	1553	78/868	4/1978
DC4035	1554	78/869	4/1978
DC4041	1555	78/870	5/1978

Class DC (continued)

Road number	Pre-TMS	Maker's numbers	Date in service
DC4058	1556	78/871	7/1978
DC4064	1557	78/872	7/1978
DC4070	1558	78/873	8/1978
DC4087	1559	78/874	8/1978
DC4093	1560	78/875	9/1978
DC4104	1561	78/876	10/1978
DC4110	1562	78/877	9/1978
DC4127	1563	78/878	12/1978
DC4133	1564	78/879	10/1978
DC4156	1565	78/880	10/1978
DC4162	1566	78/881	11/1978
DC4179	1567	78/882	12/1978
DC4185	1568	78/883	12/1978
DC4191	1569	78/884	12/1978
DC4202	1570	78/885	4/1979
DC4219	1571	78/886	2/1979
DC4225	1572	78/887	2/1979
DC4231	1573	79/888	4/1979
DC4248	1574	79/889	3/1979
DC4254	1575	79/890	2/1979
DC4260	1576	79/891	5/1979
DC4277	1577	79/892	5/1979
DC4283	1578	79/893	5/1979
DC4300	1579	79/894	6/1979
DC4317	1580	79/895	7/1979
DC4323	1581	79/896	7/1979
DC4346	1582	79/897	9/1979
DC4352	1583	79/898	8/1979
DC4369	1584	79/899	10/1979
DC4375	1585	79/900	9/1979
DC4381	1586	79/927	9/1979
DC4398	1587	79/928	10/1979
DC4409	1588	79/929	11/1979
DC4415	1589	79/930	11/1979
DC4421	1590	79/931	12/1979
DC4438	1591	79/932	12/1979
DC4444	1592	79/933	3/1980
DC4450	1593	79/934	3/1980
DC4467	1594	79/935	4/1980
DC4473	1595	79/936	4/1980
DC4496	1596	79/937	7/1980
DC4507	1597	80/938	5/1980
DC4513	1598	80/939	5/1980
DC4536	1599	80/940	5/1980
DC4542	—	80/941	7/1980
DC4559	—	80/942	5/1980
DC4565	—	80/943	7/1980
DC4571	—	80/944	7/1980
DC4588	—	80/945	8/1980
DC4594	—	80/952	8/1980
DC4605	—	80/953	9/1980
DC4611	—	80/954	9/1980
DC4628	—	80/955	11/1980
DC4634	—	80/956	12/1980
DC4640	—	80/957	12/1980
DC4657	—	80/958	12/1980
DC4663	—	80/959	12/1980
DC4686	—	80/960	12/1980
DC4692	—	80/961	3/1981
DC4703	—	81/962	2/1981
DC4726	—	81/963	4/1981
DC4732	—	81/964	3/1981
DC4749	—	81/965	6/1981
DC4755	—	81/966	9/1981
DC4761	—	81/967	11/1981
DC4778	—	81/1110	11/1982
DC4784	—	81/1111	12/1982
DC4790	—	81/1112	2/1983
DC4801	—	81/1113	3/1983
DC4818	—	81/1114	4/1983
DC4824	—	81/1115	6/1983
DC4830	—	81/1116	7/1983
DC4847	—	82/1117	8/1983
DC4853	—	82/1118	9/1983
DC4876	—	82/1119	11/1983
NZR (Hutt)			
DC4916	—	—	8/1980
DC4922	—	—	12/1980
DC4939	—	—	3/1981
DC4945	—	—	8/1981
DC4951	—	—	12/1981

Class DF Co-Co

Total: 30

Road TMS	numbers Pre-TMS	Maker's numbers	Date in service
General Motors, Canada			
DF6006	1651	A3585	10/1979
DF6012	1652	A3586	10/1979
DF6029	1653	A3587	9/1979
DF6035	1654	A3588	11/1979
DF6041	1655	A3589	8/1979
DF6058	1656	A3590	8/1979
DF6064	1657	A3591	7/1979
DF6070	1658	A3592	9/1979
DF6087	1659	A3593	11/1979
DF6093	1660	A3594	10/1979
DF6104	1661	A3595	9/1979
DF6110	1662	A3596	10/1979
DF6127	1663	A3597	10/1979
DF6133	1664	A3598	10/1979
DF6156	1665	A3599	9/1979
DF6162	1666	A3600	8/1979
DF6179	1667	A3601	10/1979
DF6185	1668	A3602	9/1979
DF6191	1669	A3603	10/1979
DF6202	1670	A3604	9/1979
DF6219	—	A3905	2/1981
DF6225	—	A3906	2/1981
DF6231	—	A3907	2/1981
DF6248	—	A3908	2/1981
DF6254	—	A3909	2/1981
DF6260	—	A3910	2/1981
DF6277	—	A3911	2/1981
DF6283	—	A3912	2/1981
DF6300	—	A3913	2/1981
DF6317	—	A3914	2/1981

Class DBR A1A-A1A

Total: 10

Road numbers	Maker's numbers	Date in service
Clyde Engineering, South Australia		
DBR1199	80/968	10/1980
DBR1200	80/969	6/1981
DBR1213	80/970	4/1981
DBR1226	80/971	7/1981
DBR1239	80/972	11/1981
DBR1241	80/973	12/1981
DBR1254	81/974	2/1982
DBR1267	81/975	3/1982
DBR1282	82/1120	9/1982
DBR1295	82/1121	10/1982

Class DX Co-Co

Total: 48

Road TMS	numbers Pre-TMS	Maker's numbers	Date in service
General Electric, USA			
DX5016	2600	38016	11/1972
DX5022	2601	38017	11/1972
DX5039	2602	38018	11/1972
DX5045	2603	38019	11/1972
DX5051	2604	38020	11/1972
DX5068	2605	38021	11/1972
DX5074	2606	38022	11/1972
DX5080	2607	38023	11/1972
DX5097	2608	38024	11/1972
DX5108	2609	38025	11/1972
DX5114	2610	38026	11/1972
DX5120	2611	38027	11/1972
DX5137	2612	38028	11/1972
DX5143	2613	38029	11/1972
DX5166	2614	38030	11/1972
DX5172	2615	40175	12/1975
DX5189	2616	40176	12/1975
DX5195	2617	40177	12/1975
DX5206	2618	40178	12/1975
DX5212	2619	40179	1/1976
DX5229	2620	40180	2/1976
DX5235	2621	40181	1/1976
DX5241	2622	40182	1/1976
DX5258	2623	40183	2/1976
DX5264	2624	40184	2/1976
DX5270	2625	40185	2/1976
DX5287	2626	40186	2/1976
DX5293	2627	40187	2/1976
DX5304	2628	40188	2/1976
DX5310	2629	40189	3/1976
DX5327	2630	40190	8/1976
DX5333	2631	40191	3/1976
DX5356	2632	40192	9/1976
DX5362	2633	40193	4/1976
DX5379	2634	40194	3/1976
DX5385	2635	40195	4/1976
DX5391	2636	40196	4/1976
DX5402	2637	40197	9/1976
DX5419	2638	40198	5/1976
DX5425	2640	40200	5/1976
DX5431	2641	40201	7/1976
DX5448	2642	40202	7/1976
DX5454	2643	40203	5/1976
DX5460	2644	40204	7/1976
DX5477	2645	40205	6/1976
DX5483	2646	40206	7/1976
DX5500	2647	40207	8/1976
DX5517	2648	40208	8/1976

Mainline electric locomotives

Class 30 Bo-Bo-Bo

Total: 22

Road numbers	Maker's numbers	Date in service
Brush Electrical Machines Ltd		
30007	876	10/1988
30013	877	1/1988
30036	878	1/1988
30042	879	2/1988
30059	880	2/1988
30065	881	3/1988
30071	882	2/1988
30088	883	2/1988
30094	884	3/1988
30105	885	11/1988
30111	886	2/1988
30128	887	3/1988
30134	888	3/1988
30140	889	5/1988
30157	890	3/1988
30163	891	5/1988
30186	892	7/1988
30192	894	10/1988
30203	893	10/1988
30226	895	9/1988
30232	896	4/1988
30249	897	2/1989

Bibliography

Cameron, W.N. *A Line of Railway*, New Zealand Railway and Locomotive Society, 1976

Cooper, Neill J. *Preserved NZR Locomotives and Railcars*, New Zealand Railway and Locomotive Society, 1982

Cousins, K.L. (Ken) & M.W. (Bill). *Pictorial Railways of New Zealand*, Cass Publications

Dyer, Peter F. *Jubilee Selections from the New Zealand Railway Observer*, New Zealand Railway and Locomotive Society, 1969

Leitch, D. & Stott, Bob. *New Zealand Railways: The First 125 Years*, Heinemann Reed, 1988

McClare, E.J. *New Zealand Railways: Diesels*, Southern Press, 1980

McGavin, Tom A. *NZR Locomotives and Railcars 1990*, New Zealand Railway and Locomotive Society, 1990

McNicol, Steve. *N.Z.R. Locomotives*, Railmac Publications, 1981

McNicol, Steve. *New Zealand Rail Scene*, Railmac Publications, 1988

Marshall, John. *Guinness Rail: The Records*, Guinness, 1985

Palmer, A.N. & Stewart, W.W. *Cavalcade of New Zealand Locomotives*, A.H. & A.W. Reed, 1965

Pickering, A.J. *Pioneer Electrics*, Tramway Historical Society, 1970

Pierre, Bill. *North Island Main Trunk: An Illustrated History*, A.H. & A.W. Reed, 1981

Sinclair, Roy. *Rail: The Great New Zealand Adventure*. Grantham House, 1987

Stott, Bob. *New Zealand Trains in Colour*, Southern Press, 1985

Troup, Gordon. *Steel Roads of New Zealand: An Illustrated Survey*, A.H. & A.W. Reed, 1973

Various Copies of the *New Zealand Railway Observer*, New Zealand Railway and Locomotive Society

Various copies of *New Zealand Model Railway Journal*, New Zealand Model Railway Guild